This is a simple and straightforward illustrated primer on a pastime which is absorbing and inexpensive. Most people think that broken china can only be mended professionally, but the author (who has mended over one thousand pieces by the methods described in this book) shows very clearly that this is not so and that anyone can, after practice and with the right materials, mend and restore china to perfection.

The book covers everything a beginner could possibly need to know, including which materials and tools to use and where to buy them. Details of all types of common repairs are concisely described and clearly illustrated in sequences of photographs, and line drawings clarify points where necessary.

This is the only book on modern methods of china mending.

This book is published by Garnstone Press, London, who issue a wide range of attractive non-fiction titles in the fields of hobbies, history, communications, literature, philosophy, London information and travel. Their catalogue is always available free on request.

Mending and Restoring China

Thomas Pond

Garnstone Press

Mending and Restoring China
is published by
Garnstone Press Limited
59 Brompton Road, London S W 3

© Thomas Pond 1970
© Illustrations: Garnstone Press Ltd 1970

ISBN: 0 900391 46 4

Printed by A. Wheaton & Co., Exeter

CONTENTS

INTRODUCTION

This volume is not intended as a comprehensive textbook but as a condensed primer of limited scope on a hobby that is useful, cheap and, if you want to make it so, profitable. Above all it is absorbing and satisfying.

I took it up almost by accident. A friend I commissioned to offer 20/– for Lot 15 at a local auction room bought Lot 20 for 15/–. This happened to be an early Bow china figure, but it was broken. When it had been professionally repaired, for £3, I sold it to a dealer as a restored piece for £35. I then decided to try china mending for myself but could find no satisfactory book on the subject or even where to buy appropriate materials. However after a year I had the opportunity to apprentice myself to a professional china restorer and during the year that followed I made real progress. I realised that, as a chemical engineer, I was applying my own specialised knowledge of solvents and plastics to the techniques I had learned, inventing new methods and substituting new materials for old.

In 1963 a 5 guinea book was published on china mending, and of its 420 pages over half were devoted to riveting and doweling. I have found riveting difficult and unsatisfactory and have always avoided it. In fact my greatest pleasure is to extract all rivets and re-mend and restore with modern glues, which were not at the disposal of restorers until ten years ago.

There is one point I would like to stress. I have had the choice of dealing superficially with many cases or describing a few in full detail. I have chosen the latter approach because the techniques described, with average application, will be equally applicable to 99% of the 'patients' that come to you. You will find descriptions of the tools and materials I have used, which does not mean that there are not other tools, materials, and indeed methods that are just as good, but simply that I think the methods I suggest are the easiest by which to work, and I cannot vouch for any others.

So I wish you pleasure and success in a new field—provided only that you can assure yourself that the skills you developed with your fingers in your schooldays are still with you, that you are not colour blind and, lastly, that you have ample patience. No patience, no china mending.

T.P.

CHAPTER ONE

CHOICE OF MATERIALS

Historical—Adhesives—Solvents—Constructional Materials—General Aids—Colours—White—Gold—Tools

HISTORICAL

In china mending shellac is still used as a constructional material. It softens in very hot water and in a small flame, is easy to shape with the fingers and very easy to rub down with sandpaper or a file, but its adhesion is relatively poor and whatever grade you buy it is very dark. I recently found that the horn of a repaired china cow was crimson underneath its paint, and it proved to be made of sealing wax, but here again the adhesion on smooth surfaces is very bad. Then again I have seen a countryman's stick replaced by a pipe cleaner, and a violin, $1\frac{1}{4}$ inches long, failed to break when the porcelain musician lost both arms and his head because somebody had gone to the trouble of carving a perfect model out of beechwood.

Although there is no doubt about the efficiency of the older glues, based on animal and fish membranes, they are not the best for mending china. Some of them smell and most of them are dark and they all soften in hot water or under the influence of heat. Visit any Do-It-Yourself shop and you will see over a dozen different plastic glues on display. Of these I suggest the following for all the jobs that may come along.

ADHESIVES

UHU. This is the trade name of a general purpose adhesive which has all round advantages. It has an excellent

1

delivery nozzle, it sticks anything very quickly indeed and is absolutely water white in colour. If you do attempt glass repairs, which are not within the scope of this book, then use Uhu. Although made in Germany, it is readily available in any hardware shop over here in two sizes at 2/6 (12½ p) and 3/9 (19 p). Get the larger size.

Epoxy Glues. This is not a trade name but the generic name for the type of resin plastic from which the glues are made. They are produced in many countries and are all the same in principle. They are sold in pairs of tubes, called twinpacks, from which equal lengths of the glue and its hardener should be squeezed on to a $3'' \times 4''$ piece of window glass. Only squeeze out sufficient for your needs for the next half hour, because once mixed (with a palette knife on the glass) a chemical reaction starts. The substance turns from a sticky liquid, through a toffee stage, to a solid, and develops its excellent adhesive properties. Sufficient strength for your purpose will be reached after twelve hours, but maximum strength develops only after a week, unless heat is applied. If an electric lamp is placed close to the glued join its heat will be sufficient to reduce the hardening time to two hours if you are in a hurry, but full details are given with each twinpack.

The strength of these epoxy glues is remarkable and I relate the following to convince you. If you take a steel bar with the diameter of an ordinary broomstick, cut through it and stick it together as per the instructions, you can hang it up and suspend from a hook at the bottom 25 grown men or 4 Morris 1100 cars. Indeed, I have seen it used from 56 lb kegs for assembling hovercraft.

However, I should point out that the strength of these glues constitutes their chief disadvantage to the china mender because once the glue is really set you cannot break the join nor can you clean the break thoroughly to start again. In fact, if you try, the odds are on breaking the porcelain in a different place. Before the glue is set ethyl alcohol is the recognised solvent, and in the toffee stage, which lasts for up to twelve hours after use, when there is adhesion but little strength, immersion in acetone will enable you to clean the join and start again. But once it is fully set there is nothing that will dissolve an epoxy glue, or at least nothing on the market, though I suspect that long term washing with household detergent may eventually break it down.

The choice of epoxy resin depends on the circumstances. When I can obtain a supply from Germany I use Uhu Plus which I have not found on the market in this country. Three English equivalents are called Araldite, Bostik 7 and Power Pack, all of which are much darker in colour—a kind of dirty grey-green—and unfortunately much more viscous and difficult to spread. However, I confess that I use any of them for all purposes quite happily. Another useful epoxy glue is called Devcon 2 Ton and is made in Canada but can be bought from two distributors in London; Messrs. Buck & Ryan Limited, 101 Tottenham Court Road, W 1 and General Engineers Supply Co, Limited, 555 High Road, Leytonstone, E 11. Both its resin and its hardener are white and opaque, like a bath enamel. It is easy to imagine how useful this can be—for filling in cracks in figures or plates, for example.

It has been said that epoxy glues can cause dermatitis, but I have used them for ten years, getting them on my fingers and making putty with them by rolling fillers into them in the palm of my hand with my forefinger, and have never had any trouble of this sort, though I am always careful to clean my hands with alcohol when I have finished work, if only because the glue is uncomfortable when it sets.

SOLVENTS

Apart from a half-pint medicine bottle full of

3

water handy on your work bench, there are four essential solvents, and you would be wise to start off with 1 pint sized bottles of each.

Alcohol. This is the solvent for epoxy resins. It is not used with the resin but simply for cleaning palette knives, tools, pieces of glass (unless you consider them expendable), the fingers, the bench and anywhere else the resin may have lodged. If you do not clean up with solvent today then you will have some scraping to do tomorrow. Alcohol can be bought in two forms—methylated spirit at 1/7 (8 p) per pint from a hardware shop, or surgical spirit at 4/5 (22 p) per pint from a chemist. They are both 90% alcohol and I have no idea why one costs more than the other. Both contain, by law, small quantities of other substances to make them undrinkable. Personally I do not like the smell of the $\frac{1}{2}$% of Pyridene that is put in the former, so I buy surgical spirit.

White Spirit. This is otherwise known as turpentine substitute and is available from a hardware shop at 1/6 (7$\frac{1}{2}$ p) per pint. It is used as a solvent for other materials, but principally for oil colours, both for making them up and for cleaning them off.

Acetone. This is essential for removing cellulose car paints from brushes. A small supply can be found in a bottle of nail varnish remover, a larger supply must come from a chemist's shop. As already mentioned, it is used for the emergency removal of epoxy resins.

Xylene. There is an excellent impact adhesive called Evostick, which is not suitable for this work, but some repairers do use it and should you wish to re-stick a piece that has been mended in this way you will find it difficult to clean off. Xylene removes it at once. Benzole or Benzene can be used in place of Xylene and, failing these, National Benzole Mixture.

4

CONSTRUCTIONAL MATERIALS

Kaolin. Epoxy resin can be used not only as a glue but, when compounded with Kaolin, as a mouldable epoxy putty. This can be bought from a chemist at 2/6 (12½ p) per lb. A half-pound packet will last for a long time. Try to get a grade which is really white, like Plaster-of-Paris, because some grades are an unpleasant grey colour. The other well known filling material is titanum oxide (Titanox) which is as true a white as exists and is the basis for all modern white paints. However, I find that it makes a stickier putty than Kaolin and I prefer Kaolin in spite of its inferior colour which, in any case, is almost invariably hidden under a coat of paint.

Seel-Masta. Recently this material has been marketed in two tins at 6/6 (32½ p) the pair. It is recommended for various purposes, including the making of figurines, for which it is excellent. It is basically an epoxy resin with the hardener in the other tin, already containing fillers, similar to an epoxy putty made with Kaolin or Titanox. After mixing it can be rolled thin or shaped and it supports its own weight very well. It saves all the work of preparing putty, and is far less sticky, though there are disadvantages. One is the putty's relatively poor adhesive qualities. It does not hold on to a shell break at the edge of a plate, for example, and a flower made with it has to be stuck in place with another adhesive. Secondly, the mixing has to be very thorough and therefore takes rather a long time.

Polyester Resins These are commonly referred to as fibre-glass resins and a convenient pack, available in all hardware or DIY shops, is called Isopon.

Isopon. This consists of a tin of grey paste, a small tube or bottle of orange coloured catalyst and about a square foot of glass fibre, and it costs about 12/- (60 p). It is unlikely that you will require more glass fibre than this, so on re-ordering buy the refill and not the whole kit. The catalyst is dyed orange to assist you in judging when the two substances are properly mixed. Full instructions are given with each pack and it is an easy material to work, on which a perfect finish can be obtained without difficulty.

However, there are three important points which the instructions do not make clear. (1) One drop of orange catalyst will harden a teaspoonful of Isopon in about ten minutes, and four drops in about three minutes. Trial will show you that the speed of hardening is entirely controllable. (2) If the thick liquid Isopon hardens to a crumbly texture, do not proceed. Make a fresh mix using less catalyst. (3) It is not possible to add coloured paints to Isopon, as you can to epoxy putty or Seelmasta, without destroying its strength. You must use surface colouring only.

When you have mixed the Isopon on a piece of glass, heap it up with a palette knife to the shape and thickness of the article you are going to make. It is very tacky and impossible to work at this stage. Wait. In a few minutes it will cease to flow out of the form you have given it and will become rubbery. Now trim it to the approximate shape of the article you want, discarding the offcuts. Remove the crude shape from the glass with a palette knife and continue to trim it with a razor blade, while holding it in the hand. Note that you have only a few minutes for this work after which the Isopon will become rock hard and have to be finished with a file and wet-and-dry paper.

I recommend Isopon for making small pieces that must be finished accurately in the geometrical sense (a bow and arrow, for example) rather than in the sculptured sense (an arm or a leg). Incidentally, this is the material from which lorry cabs and dinghies are made, and with which car wings and bodies are repaired. It can be filed, drilled, tapped etc.

Barbola. This is an old established art school material for building flowers etc., and cannot be bettered. A large tin, which contains about 1 lb and costs 6/- (30 p), is the size to buy. Be careful how you put the lid back after use because in my opinion it is too flimsy and if it becomes distorted, or if it is left off altogether, the Barbola goes hard and has to be softened with water before use, which is troublesome and messy. After I have dug out and used the middle I stick a small sponge in the middle of the lid which I keep moist. The Barbola then remains in perfect condition.

Gesso is a mixture of carpenter's glue and Whiting or Plaster of Paris and is used for the moulded design on large picture frames. It is the basis of papier mâché. Personally, I prefer Isopon for repairing the rims of papier mâché trays because it is far less messy, and sets more quickly.

Plaster-of-Paris. You can get this from most chemists and a 1 lb packet should suffice. It is the freshness that matters, the colour does not as you will only use it for moulding and supporting purposes.

Paribar. This is a brown gum used by dentists for taking moulds of the teeth. It has a very narrow softening range in hot water. Beware of leaving it unattended in water over a flame because if it is heated beyond its softening point it becomes liquid, sticking to the bottom of the pan. Once this has happened it is almost impossible to remove it, even when chilled and rehardened. It is in any case wiser to use an old tin for this purpose than a saucepan. Paribar is useful for copying little pieces that have been lost, so long as there is an identical one to work from. Two pieces, $3'' \times 3''$, will probably last your lifetime, because you can re-use it as often as you like. It is not difficult to manipulate and one trial will show you how to deal with it. Cover the front and sides of the object to be copied, but leave the back clear. While it is still mouldable press the material firmly onto the object,

7

so that it touches each surface. In less than a minute you will be able to remove the mould—with the aid of a hot knife blade if necessary.

Plasticine. A packet of children's plasticine can be bought for 6d (2½ p) or 1/- (5 p) in any toy shop. If I had to state which is the most important of all the tools I have in my workshop, I should have to nominate plasticine, unbelieveable as it may sound. There are four pieces in various stages of rehabilitation in my workshop at the time of writing, and on all of them something is being supported by plasticine. When you press, it gives, and when you stop pressing it remains in exactly the same position, never moving a fraction of an inch.

COLOURS

Gold. One small bottle of yellow gold and one small bottle of red gold, from an art shop, will last for years. Mixed in various proportions with picture varnish they will give any of the whole range of gold colours and the result lasts well. It does not give the burnished effect of real gold leaf, but the application of gold leaf is an art in itself—it is not as expensive as it sounds, nor is it easy. It is not something that can be described, but must be taught by someone who really understands the art. However, it is only on broad surfaces that the comparatively rough surface of the paint shows up badly— carefully applied in thin lines it answers the problem very well.

Treasure Gold. This is another material which is worth mentioning in this context. It is an American product but sold in this country in art shops and comes in three tones. Choose the middle one. It is expensive—a small pot costs about £1 (£1.00)—but it lasts a long time if you always put the lid back after use. Antique dealers use it for touching up the gold on picture frames. I have always applied it by rubbing it onto the surface with one finger. The body heat seems to be just enough to melt the wax of which it is composed. It is excellent for large surfaces, but my advice is to be sure you need it before you rush out to buy it.

White. This can be made to sound a formidably difficult subject, and indeed it can be, but there are ways of getting round it. The problem is that the white of porcelain varies considerably. The glaze on Delft china is always blue, for instance, that on Chinese porcelain blue or blue-green, but the majority of pieces are glazed in yellow ochre. To match these you will need Flake White. You can buy a medium sized tube from an art shop or you can buy it in powder form and, using a palette knife, mix it with some drops of picture varnish and enough white spirit to make it flow on application. The latter is the cheaper way, the former the more convenient, but there is little in it. It can be mixed with other colours to produce the exact shade required.

However, for the larger plain white surfaces I recommend car touch-up paint. Polar white, Arctic white and a pale ivory are the most useful and can be bought from most large garages. A stroke of each on a thin piece of metal sheet make an excellent matching card to place against the area you have to cover. These paints are made to stand up to wind, sun and rain and keep their tone well. I do not recommend Joy for this purpose because I find that it turns brown rather quickly and is too thick. These touch-up paints cost 5/6 (27½ p) a tin and have a little brush in the lid which is very convenient. Be careful, though, not to let the paint get into the outside threads of the neck of the tin, because the plastic top will break if it sticks and you have to try and force it open.

I will go into the method of application of these paints later, but they require their own solvent, acetone, for cleaning the brushes. Be careful of acetone, it is very volatile and very inflammable.

Colours. As you will use such very small quantities of coloured paints you should buy the smallest tubes available in students' quality which are about 1/6 (7½ p) each in an art shop. The important ones are:

Burnt Sienna	Chrome Yellow	Flake White
Flesh Tint	Madder Rose	Payne's Grey
Ultramarine	Vandyck Brown	Vermilion
Viridian	Windsor Blue	Yellow Ochre

Orange, Violet and Terre Verte can be added but are not essential.

Picture Varnish. This is the medium used for colouring the finished repair, when mixed with the required colour. It is also used to give the final gloss or glaze when this is necessary. I recommend Rowneys No. 800 Clear, which is non-blooming and retains its water-white colour indefinitely. It is freely miscible with white spirit, which you should use for thinning it if necessary.

Sandpaper. Sandpaper and glasspaper are much the same and are produced in several grades. Choose a sheet of medium-coarse and a sheet of medium-fine. They are used for smoothing any of the hard materials mentioned above. Fold the paper both ways before you tear it and use very small pieces—large ones are unwieldy.

Wet-and-Dry Paper. This is something different. Although it can be used as sandpaper it is most effective when it has been dipped in water. In this condition it must not, of course, be used on Barbola, but it produces a very smooth surface on an epoxy putty. Choose two sheets of coarse and a sheet of fine. Once again, use very small pieces. When you have achieved what you consider to be a satisfactory smooth surface with the coarse wet-and-dry paper, work on the same surface for just fifteen seconds with the fine for a really perfect finish.

Tools. You will no doubt collect your own tools with experience, but you will need the following:

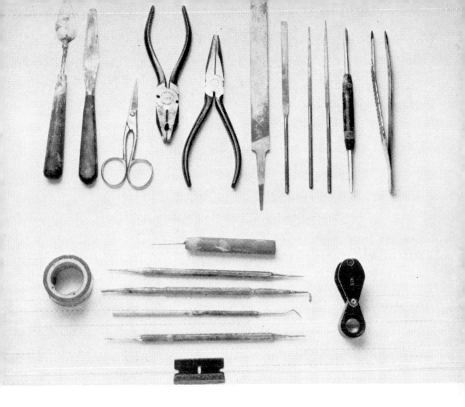

Plate 2

6″ (overall) triangular palette knife—shaped like a trowel	7/6	(37½ p)
6″ (overall) straight edge palette knife	7/6	(37½ p)
6″ (overall) trowel-shaped palette knife (blade only ¾″ long and ½″ wide at its broadest. No. 19 Alsons. Made in Italy. Available in most art shops).	8/6	(42½ p)
Pair of scissors—about 3″		
Pair of broad nosed pliers, containing wire cutters, about 6″	6/-	(30 p)
Pair of long nosed pliers, 6″ overall	6/-	(30 p)
Flat coarse-cut file with 6″ blade	4/-	(30 p)
Flat fine-cut file with 4″ blade	4/-	(30 p)
Set of small locksmith's files which must include triangular, square and rat-tail	8/-	(40 p)

11

Roll of Sellotape   2/-   (10 p)
Magnifying glass up to 15 magnification
Can of 1 in 3 lubricating oil   2/-   (10 p)
Pieces of window glass (about 4″ × 3″)
Everready blades, used or unused
Cotton wool and clean rags
Wet-and-dry abrasive paper—coarse and
    fine
Sandpaper—coarse and fine

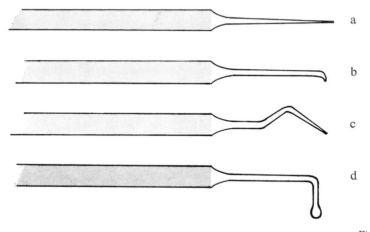

a

b

c

d

Fig. 1

You should also try to get hold of the following if possible:

The dentist's tools illustrated in Fig. 1
A pair of dentist's tweezers
1 foot of thin lead pipe—see Fig. 2
A piece of 5 ply board, about 12″ × 7″, to act as a turn-
    table
A block of wood, about 6″ × 4″ × 3″
An open topped box, approximately 12″ × 8″ × 4″,
    containing 3″ of sand, to act as a rest box.

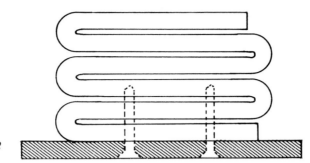

Fig. 2

Where to buy

You will find that all the materials I have recommended are readily available from local chemists, art shops or Do-it-Yourself shops.

The common household tools can be bought in almost any hardware shop or ironmongers.

A hardware shop will probably stock lead piping—a builder's merchant certainly will, though I admit I would feel a fool going into the latter for one foot of lead pipe.

For the wood I would recommend a Do-it-Yourself shop, although a wood merchant might be able to help because the small pieces you need are only off-cuts and throw-outs.

The dentist's tools (and the Paribar) are available new from Claudius Ash, 26–40 Broadwick Street, W1A 2AD or 23a St Thomas Street, S E 1. This same firm has branches in Belfast, Birmingham, Bournemouth, Brighton, Bristol, Canterbury, Cardiff, Edinburgh, Leeds, Liverpool, Manchester, Newcastle, Nottingham, Plymouth and Southampton. However, these tools have no second-hand value, so it is always worthwhile asking your own dentist if he has any discarded ones available.

13

CHAPTER TWO

WHY TO AVOID RIVETING AND DOWELING

When I started mending china I bought a diamond, clamped it in a nail, built a very efficient Chinese native drill with bamboo and string with which I could drill very neat holes in porcelain—and never used it to rivet a repair.

I will go further and state that my greatest pleasure now is to find a riveted plate, file through the centres of all the rivets, lever them out, plug the holes with Devcon 2 Ton putty and stick the plate together again. (See Plate 3).

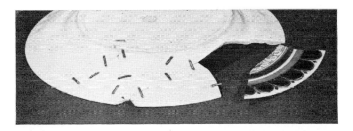

Plate 3a

Plate 3b

The single rivet has been left in solely for identification purposes.

One must in all fairness admit that before the days of these glues of great strength there was no alternative to riveting, but it had three great disadvantages. First, it is an extremely unsightly method, secondly no riveted jug or cup can hold liquid, and thirdly, rivets are not permanent. Under tension, as they always are, the brass of which they are made loses its spring and they become loose.

With epoxy resins one can now stick together a 20″ meat dish which would otherwise need at least twenty rivets. Lids of modern earthenware oven dishes are common household casualties and, on the face of it, suitable patients for riveting. But they are easily repaired invisibly with epoxy glues so long as they are not put into a very hot oven. (If the dish is used for cooking in the oven, even if you have scrupulously removed all excess glue, a brown line will appear all along the repair with the heat. But even so the lid will be perfectly sound.)

If by doweling is meant the boring of two holes and the insertion of a connecting wire dowel, then I am equally against it. Modern glues are strong and do not need this kind of assistance. If by chance you come across a figure which is hollow in the neck or the limbs, so that there are two matching rings to be stuck, you can whittle down a piece of soft wood, tapered to the shape of the holes, and insert this when you make the join, but it is quite unnecessary and may even complicate the job.

On the other hand, putting a peg on to a broken surface and building a new limb around it must not be confused with doweling, and is a very practical measure.

If I seem to have dismissed rather briefly two old-established methods of china mending, it must be remembered that methods do become obsolete. When a method whose result is neither beautiful nor effective is also laborious and difficult to carry out it seems only sensible to discard it altogether.

CHAPTER THREE

FIRST PRINCIPLES

Cleanliness—Glue Quantity—Resting Positions—Supports

Before I describe some individual repairs, there are certain basic principles I should mention. They are all quite obvious, and easy to carry out, but none the less essential.

CLEANLINESS

Examine both the surfaces to be brought together to make sure that they are absolutely clean, often of other repairers' unsuccessful efforts. A magnifying glass is essential for this. Remember that the object is to make the join as nearly invisible as possible with the minimum amount of glue. If you can see coloured spots on one of the surfaces of the break, they must be removed. If the adhesion of a previous repair was bad, it is possible that one edge will be dirty and the other clean. Examine the 'clean' edge all the same.

Fig. 3

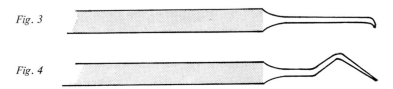

Fig. 4

Some of the colourless cellulose acetate glues (which I do not recommend) peel off in long strips quite easily. Some glues dissolve in hot water or in white spirit, in alcohol or acetone. A glue which no solvent will remove is probably an epoxy glue, and in this case you will have to use sandpaper or else chip the residue away with a dentists' pick. (See Fig. 3). Sometimes you can hear the difference between glue and porcelain when you move over it with the point of the probe (see Fig. 4) even when it is not visible to the naked eye.

It is essential to remove every scrap of old glue before embarking on a repair, since it is clearly impossible for two surfaces to meet smoothly when a foreign body, however minute, is present on one of them.

GLUE QUANTITY

Be as mean as you dare with glue application. This is not a question of economy, although there is no point in wasting glue. One reason for this is that the strongest join is the one with the least glue left in it. Also, you should examine the join as soon as you have made it, and if you have to clear away a ring of excess glue before you can see what you have achieved it is quite likely that you will move the pieces and spoil your careful handiwork. Finally, imagine that you are repairing a large plate, the middle portion of which is entire, but the rim of which is in twenty pieces. Suppose that you use 1/100th of an inch thickness of glue instead of a fine smear, when you come to the last piece you will have in the rim twenty 1/100ths thickness of glue, which is nearly a quarter of an inch. This means that if the last piece to be fitted is an inch wide, you will find that a quarter of it will not go in.

In this book I continually harp on the thinnest possible application of epoxy glues. Now, having mentioned the possibility, remote in my opinion, of dermatitis, I feel constrained to tell you how I apply these glues and allow you to make your own decision. Having put tiny dabs of glue along the edge of a break, with a palette knife, I spread them, to form a continuous layer, with even pressure from my forefinger. (Remember that broken edges of porcelain can be sharp. However, if you are careful there is no reason why you should cut yourself). The excess either comes off on my finger, in which case I spread it on the other edge as far as it will go, or else it goes over the edge, in which case it can be wiped off with a rag (as it can from the finger). In this way I avoid the excess glue which is so troublesome to remove. If you decide that you don't want to touch the glue in this way then you must carry out the whole operation with a palette knife.

RESTING POSITIONS

Before you begin work, it is wise to prepare a suitable resting place for the piece you are going to mend. You will find a wooden box, four inches deep, of a size convenient to your work space and containing three inches of dry sand, convenient as far as cups, figures, small plates etc. are concerned. During the setting period it is essential that gravity is considered, that the join is horizontal to the ground, and that any tendency for the pieces to slide one over the other is eliminated as far as possible. For instance, a cup on which the handle is being replaced should be put on its side, one third immersed in the sand, with the handle in a vertical position. However, for delicate final adjustments it is difficult to work over a box and in these cases it is wise to make individual supports for everything.

Fig. 5

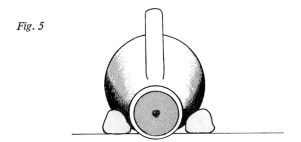

Plates and dishes I place vertically in a drawer of my work desk, (see Fig. 6) shutting the drawer as far as is necessary to hold the object steady. I support a cup with two peas of plasticine pushed into the gaps between the cup and the bench on either side to stop it rolling. (See Fig. 5.) It is for this support difficulty that I find plasticine of such great value.

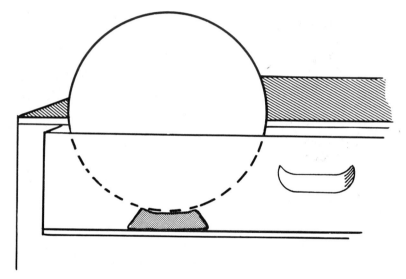

Fig. 6

One of the most difficult things I have ever repaired was an old glazed earthenware ladle, whose shank was snapped in the middle. (See Fig. 7). It was necessary to prepare a bed of plasticine along both parts of the

Fig. 7

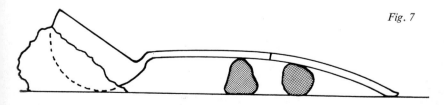

broken shank before even selecting the adhesive. Although it takes more time, it is wise in this situation to make a support base for the ladle bowl itself. I used a Plaster-of-Paris mould, similar to the one shown around the cup in Plate 4. This made it possible to manipulate the shank into its exact position once the glue had been applied. It is wise to set up this kind of job on a piece of blockboard. The whole thing can then be turned round and the other side examined.

Plate 4

You will have gathered that some ingenuity is necessary in preparing the support and resting position, which varies in every case. I would also strongly advise you not to try to make two joins in the same piece at the same time if they are going to be difficult to manage, and never. never try two mends at once if the joins are not both going to be horizontal.

21

SUPPORTS

These are so important to the china mender that they merit a section to themselves. The following are examples which will be a useful guide, and can be adapted to suit individual cases.

1.   A block of wood, an offcut from a builder's yard, $6'' \times 4'' \times 3''$ is very useful. Depending on which way you stand it up, you have a choice of three different heights from which to arrange supports.

2.   Wooden skewers from a poulterer's, stuck to one of the sides of the block with plasticine, will reach places otherwise difficult to support. (See Fig. 8.)

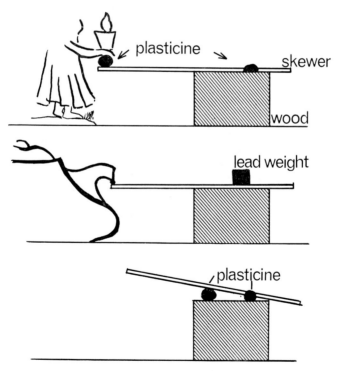

Fig. 8

3. Sometimes it is necessary to exert slight pressure on a newly replaced limb during hardening. This is often done by means of two tiny polythene bags of sand or lead shot, tied at the necks and connected with a piece of string.

4. A piece of $\frac{3}{4}''$ lead pipe, about 8″ long, hammered flat and bent as shown in Fig. 2 can be fastened with a couple of nails to a small piece of plywood to make a compact and useful weight. Tie a piece of string round it and loop the string over an object to exert pressure over a small area.

5. Similarly, when hammered round a skewer (see Fig. 9) and then stuck to a small piece of plywood with epoxy glue, it forms a very stable support for another skewer held crosswise, and if necessary at an angle, with a piece of plasticine.

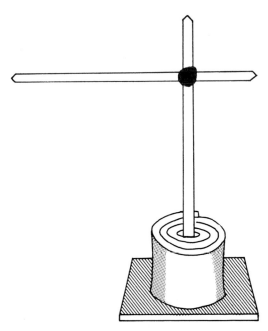

Fig. 9

6. Three such supports are invaluable for repairing the stem of a tall wine glass, where 100% accuracy is essential. These supports can all be dismantled by removing the plasticine and used again on other occasions at different angles. (See Plate 5.)

Plate 5

7. To ensure that leaves or petals made of epoxy putty or Seelmasta assume a live form, a ring or lump of plasticine can be placed near the point of application and the pliable putty allowed to droop over it. (See Fig. 10.) Once the putty is set the plasticine can be removed.

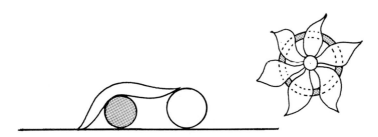

Fig. 10

8. In the case of the broken cup in Plate 4, you will realise that it is extremely difficult to hold a curving slope, broken in this way, in position while the glue sets. The answer is first to cover the unbroken side of the cup with a light smear of oil or vaseline. Then pour a $\frac{1}{4}''$ thick layer of Plaster-of-Paris over this side of the cup, covering an area greater than that of the pieces you have to replace (but less than half the circumference of the cup, or you will not be able to remove the mould). Allow the Plaster-of-Paris to continue towards the base, so that it covers the rim on which the cup stands and even a little of the base itself. When the Plaster-of-Paris is set, slide the mould around the cup to cover the gap and fix it in position with sellotape. You can now stick the pieces into position with comparative ease, holding the cup at any convenient angle, because the replaced pieces have something to lean on.

CHAPTER FOUR

MENDING AND RESTORING

Simple Joins—Multi-Breaks—Small Missing Pieces—
Filling in Holes—Shell Breaks—Replacement of Missing
Objects—Tea Pot Spouts—Replacing a Cup Handle

SIMPLE JOINS

Here are details of the procedure I would follow when replacing a limb broken from a small figure, using epoxy resin. (While Uhu is quick and easy to use, suitable for figurines, and even for plates providing they are for decorative purposes only, an epoxy resin is nevertheless stronger and worth the extra trouble. It is essential for replacing objects such as cup handles, which have to support weight, or for repairing plates that are to be used.)

1. Prepare a suitable rest bed.

2. From one of the twin pack tubes squeeze onto a piece of glass $\frac{1}{8}''$ of glue. Replace the cap at once, for two good reasons. One is that if you do not resin may continue to ooze out after you have put the tube down. The other is that you must next squeeze a similar portion from the other tube and you may put the caps back on the wrong tubes. If you do, the resins mixing in the caps will start their chemical reaction and the next time you want to use the glue you will find that both caps are immovable.

3. With the point of the small palette knife, mix the two portions thoroughly until they become cloudy. Should you for any reason wish to add a third constituent, such as a pigment or dye, do this after the original mixing.

4. Cover both surfaces to be joined with the minimum amount of glue, carried in minute portions

on the tip of the palette knife. Wipe both sides of the palette knife on the edge of the glass, scrape up the residue and return it to the main pile. Then, with the palette knife, scrape off any excess glue from both sides of the join, returning it, as before, to the pile. In effect one really needs to grease the surfaces and no more.

5.   Fix clearly in your mind exactly how the pieces fit together, using a broken piece of pattern, if there is one, or a jagged point in the fracture, to judge by, and bring the pieces together. If you are holding the pieces so that the join is horizontal they will hold together long enough for you to change the position of one hand. There is an obvious point I feel I should emphasize here. There is only ONE position in which the two pieces will join perfectly, and you have got to find it, sometimes by joggling the two pieces about until you do. The microscopic depressions have got to be filled by their corresponding bumps, or, to some degree, the gap on the outside will yawn.

6.   Press the pieces together as firmly as you dare, and how good or bad your application of glue has been will now become apparent. Set the object down on its prepared rest bed and examine it. This is where a piece of blockboard will come in very useful, if you have made the rest bed on it, because it may be necessary to examine the back of the repair as well. It is as well not to touch the object once it is on its rest bed, and it is often easier to turn the board round than to climb round the worktable to make an examination. This is especially true when you have to check whether or not the newly stuck piece is truly vertical, looking at it from an angle of 90 degrees.

7.   In spite of care in application, glue will probably have squeezed out in one or two places, and there are three ways of removing it:

(a) Pull it off gently with a fine point immediately, without touching the object itself.

(b) After four hours, use a small piece of cotton wool moistened (not soaked) in alcohol and held in a pair of tweezers to wipe off the excess. Do not press hard on the join.

(c) Leave the object for twelve or fifteen hours and then pare off the excess with a razor blade followed by sandpaper.

In certain cases one can use a trick to avoid the problem of excess glue. If you have to replace the head on the body of a figure and the neck is about an inch in diameter proceed as above but only apply the glue, to each surface, in a rough circle with a diameter of not more than $\frac{3}{4}''$, leaving a ring round the outside which is free of glue. When you apply the necessary pressure to put the head in position, the excess glue will flow into the empty circle and should not reach the edge.

8. Leave the figure in the rest bed, supported if and where necessary, for about three hours and then examine the join once more, running the point of the probe across it. If you find no 'step' then swab off any excess glue that has seeped out and leave the piece to set. If you do find a step, try to adjust it. If you have no success, you must break the join, clean it with spirit, and then start again.

When repairing a plate, prepare the epoxy glue as before and carry out the repair exactly as described above until you reach the point where the two edges are brought together for the first time.

In this case of a plate, the rest bed will probably be a table drawer, open just enough to hold the plate in the vertical position. (See Fig. 11.) The weight of the top portion is now bearing downwards and the top piece will not slide because the join is horizontal. Run your forefinger very lightly up the edge of the plate at A and B. If you feel a step in either place, gently slide A towards B or vice versa until the step disappears. Now for the other

29

plane. Lightly pass the point of a probe, or better still a pin, vertically across the join to see if there is a step in this direction, and adjust accordingly. Then check on the sides at A and B again to see that any movement necessary to adjust the second plane has not created problems on the other plane.

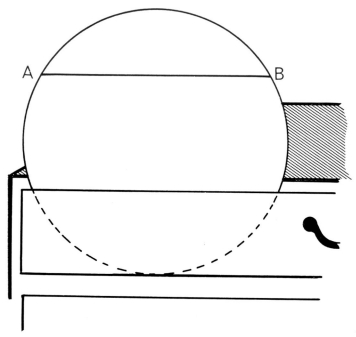

Fig. 11

Examine the join with the probe in about three hours. If you find no step, simply swab off the excess glue and leave the plate to set fully. If you do find a step, try to adjust it. It will be necessary to use more force than before. If you have no success, you will have to break the join, clean it with spirit, and start again. When you are using an epoxy glue it is important to make this check within about six hours, while it is still possible to adjust the join or remove the glue.

MULTI-BREAKS

In the case of the plate shown in (Fig. 12), do not try to stick pieces 1, 2, 3 and 4 to the main piece at one session. It rarely works. For example, stick 3 and 4 on the first day and 1 and 2 on the next day. If the plate is in twenty pieces this may be a very long job. However, this cannot be avoided because you cannot expect pieces 3 and 4 to stay in place when you are pressing hard on pieces 1 and 2 to squeeze the excess glue out. Take care to smear glue only along the edges EFG and GHI—not along EG and GI—or pieces 1 and 2 will never take up their correct places when the time comes. Similarly, when treating the big unbroken pieces be very careful not to put glue any further from F than E, i.e.: not along EZ or IX. These surfaces should be given their minimum coats when pieces 1 and 2 are to be put in.

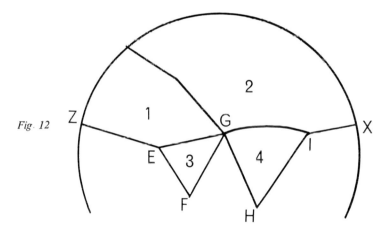

Fig. 12

There are no short cuts when you are dealing with a multi-break. For instance, if you try to glue several pieces at once and use sellotape to hold them in position while the glue sets you will find that the chemicals in the glue weaken the sellotape and it will sag and allow the pieces to slip.

SMALL MISSING PIECES

In the type of repair just discussed there is a very common complication. This is that some of the broken pieces may be hardly larger than crumbs. It is impossible to work with these minute splinters. They should be discarded and the holes filled in later. However, when the pieces are about the size of a match-head it is worth trying to put them in place, even though it is not at all easy. These pieces are often triangular and the real difficulty is to determine which is the true position of each one, as at first glance they can go in any of three ways. Here, too you may find that you have to leave a hole and fill it in in the following manner.

FILLING IN HOLES

Barbola is the best material for this, and you should try and keep it in its tin in the state of soft putty.

Put a piece the size of a pea on a strip of glass, roll it flat and cut it into strips. Moisten the edges of the hole slightly (saliva does very well for this!) take what you judge to be sufficient Barbola on the point of a probe, place it in the hole and push it firmly into place. The tool used by a dentist for pressing in fillings is ideal for this (see Fig. 13). Add more if the hole is not full,

Fig. 13

and remove excess, if necessary, either with a rag if the Barbola is soft enough, or with a razor blade if it is of a putty-like consistancy. An ordinary safety razor blade split in two lengthwise is a useful tool for this, because it will bend to the curvature of the plate or dish. If the level of the Barbola is still slightly higher than the surface, work it down with a wet finger, wiping the resultant moisture away from the filling with a rag. Leave the plate for twenty-four hours to allow the fillings to dry out thoroughly, after which it will be ready for finishing and colouring. The best way to deal with really microscopic holes is to use Barbola in a cream-like consistency, spread it over the area and wipe it off again. When the Barbola has set in the holes, clean the surface free of smears with a damp rag. If the tiny pieces are missing from the edge of the plate, treat the gaps similarly, but here the Barbola should be putty-like and a very small touch of Uhu will help it to stay in position. Allow the Barbola plenty of time to dry out. If you finish off a repair of this kind too quickly the Barbola will continue to dry under its paint and will contract and fall out of place.

SHELL BREAKS

These are ellipsoidal chips on the edges of plates. Usually the pieces have been lost. If the defect is on a decorative plate the above treatment will be satisfactory. If on a plate that is going to be used the treatment is different because it will have to stand up to frequent washing. You can either smear on the shell chip a mixture of epoxy glue and kaolin, building it up until it is slightly higher and wider than the final surface is to be, or else use Seelmasta in the same way, first covering the shell break with a very thin layer of epoxy resin. (This is because, as already mentioned, the Seelmasta alone has not sufficient adhesive power.) Whichever you choose, allow it to harden. If on later examination you find that you have used too much, pare off some of the excess with a split razor blade. This saves work when it comes to the final rubbing down with wet-and-dry paper, which must not be done until the putty is set really hard. Setting time can be considerably reduced by raising the temperature of the putty. Full details of the influence of increased temperature on setting times are given in the instructions that come with the epoxy glues, but in fact all you need to do is to place the plate (or whatever) under an Angle-poise lamp with the tip of the bulb about five inches above the glue. Experience will show you that by this means days can be reduced to the equivalent hours.

Next, cut off a piece of coarse wet-and-dry paper, about 3″ × 2″, and wet it in a dish of water. Fold it in half and rub the surface of the repair fairly hard for about fifteen seconds. Pass your finger over the surface to check the result. Wet the paper again and repeat the rubbing until you are satisfied that you have worn the putty down to the correct level and that any steps have disappeared. Check that the surface is completely smooth before attempting any form of finishing.

A word of warning must be added here. Wet-and-dry paper, which will remove hardened epoxy resin, will also remove a coloured design, unless it is protected by a heavy top glaze. Gold, for instance, is almost always surface applied, and rubbing with the wet-and-dry paper must be done with great care and only just over the area of the shell break. That is why it is wise to use a small piece of paper that can be folded even smaller.

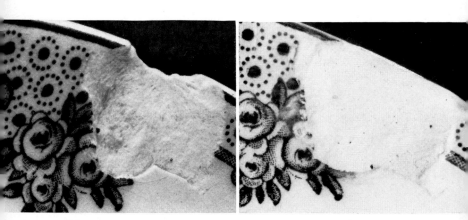

Plate 6   *Plate 7*

REPLACEMENT OF MISSING OBJECTS

Basically, there are two types of missing object, those which, when replaced, need additional support, and those which do not. This depends on size and weight. Experience soon makes this clear, but a couple of examples may help.

A flower in the basket of a four inch high flower-seller, once formed, requires no dowel support. The finial, or knob, on the lid of a sugar basin, whatever its size, efficiently replaced with epoxy glue, should be strong enough to bear the weight not only of the lid, but of the basin full of sugar as well. The outstretched arm of an 8″ figure, however, which has a basket suspended from the hand, may well require some extra support, as would the handle of a cup which has to carry hot tea.

Formerly, to give this extra support a china mender would bore a hole in the stump of the arm, or whatever it might be, and put a peg in it. Even when the existing arm was to be replaced on the stub, holes were bored to take the peg in this as well. Nowadays, modern glues render this extra support unnecessary, but sometimes it is convenient and wise to mould a new limb onto a figure with the help of a peg. In this way the peg gives support to the soft moulding material as well as eventually strengthening the repaired limb. See 'Replacing a Cup Handle' below.

TEA POT SPOUTS

There is no doubt that of all the pieces in an old tea service which is most likely to be damaged, it is the spout of the tea pot. Fortunately, they are very easy to repair.

1. It is possible that both lips will be damaged, but more usually it is the lower one and the first step is

to decide what shape it should be. If you are a purist, you will check in library books and museums, but at the very least you must make a sketch of the shape you think will look right. (See Fig. 14.)

Fig. 14

2.   Clean off as much as possible of the tannin stains, which will have permeated into the unglazed broken surfaces, by immersion in household bleach.

3.   If you have the little pieces that make up the lip, you at least know the correct shape. It is, however, far, far easier to make a new lip than to glue these broken fragments together.

4.   Mix an epoxy glue and, before adding the kaolin, smear a little glue on to the broken surfaces to assist in the keying, because the putty you make should in this case be on the dry side, which means that the adhesion is not quite so good.

5.   Place a sausage of the putty along the lip, squeezing a very little of it—not more than $\frac{1}{8}''$—back over and back under the lip. The remainder is pulled forward with the finger and thumb to form the lip itself. If the finger is dipped in kaolin and rubbed against the thumb there will be less risk of the putty tearing away from the epoxy-covered edge. With intermittent squeezing and manipulation the lip will take shape. If you find that it is thinner than the final lip should be, add a small pea of putty in the right place and squeeze it into position. If you started with too much, and the lip has extended out too far, support it with a finger of the left hand and cut off the excess to a more suitable shape with a small pair of scissors, the blades of which should also be dipped in the kaolin bottle. At the end of this stage the

lip, ideally, should be slightly larger in every dimension than the finished lip is to be. In fact, this stage is not so difficult as it may sound.

6. Some support must be given to the lip before the work is put aside to harden. This can be done with a piece of sellotape 2″ long, the middle of which touches the underneath of the lip, the ends being curled round and stuck to the original china. When the putty is set, the sellotape pulls away from it without any difficulty. If the top of the spout is also missing and there is nothing to which you can conveniently affix the sellotape, you must devise a support with the help of the information on page 22.

7. Putty of the consistency described, once set, can be worked with great ease and accuracy. Razor blade, rat-tailed file and wet-and-dry paper will be required in that order. With the razor blade pare off small slivers of hardened putty, being careful to match one side of the lip with the other. This is best done while looking at the front of the tea pot. If the blade touches the original china you will feel and hear it. Stop using the knife at once, because the last thing you want to do is to form a step.

Inside, the spout is slightly more difficult to work with the blade, so use the file, going down the throat of the spout as far as necessary. When you have obtained the shape you require, rub it down with wet-and-dry paper, first with the coarse and then with the fine. To work inside the spout, roll the wet-and-dry paper into a cylinder, or round the file.

8. If the teapot is for cabinet display only, paint with matching white, using two coats, and painting inside and out, adding gold and any other design as required. If the teapot is to have normal table use, you can finish as above but the gold along the edge will not last, and it may be better to be satisfied with glossy white.

REPLACING A CUP HANDLE

Three years ago I bought a half-pint coffee cup of Crown Derby porcelain without a handle. I fitted a new handle as described below. I have used the cup every day since and that means that over a thousand times the handle has supported a pound in weight of hot coffee on its epoxy glue joins, and it is as strong as ever. I admit, though, that it has never been washed in detergent, which is the enemy of all adhesives and paints.

1.   As always, the first step is to prepare a suitable rest bed so that you can put the cup down whenever you need a rest or to examine your work.

2.   Choose a piece of brass wire, about one third or one quarter the diameter of the cup handle that is to be made. Cut it about half an inch longer than the handle-to-be. If it is not quite straight this does not matter. With a triangular file make about ten or fifteen notches in the wire in random positions all along it. These are to act as keys for the moulding material to stop it sliding. (See Fig. 15.)

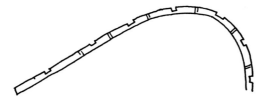

Fig. 15

3.   With a pair of pliers bend the wire of the handle-to-be. If you need to create sharp angles use two pairs of pliers. Snip off short bits from either end until the two ends, when held in their final position, touch the centre of the two porcelain stubs. It is a good idea to mark the centre points of the two stubs with pencil, as a guide, because these areas, which are often at an angle, can be quite large, and it is important that the length of the wire is correct. (See Plate 8.)

4. Mix sufficient epoxy glue and put a blob on each stub. Then put blobs of similar size on both ends of the wire. Embed the middle of the wire in a piece of plasticine, roughly cone-shaped, and place the wire in position, putting pressure on the plasticine to make it stick to the body of the cup, smearing it downwards on both sides if necessary to make it hold better. (See Plate 9.) Now adjust the final position of the wire by bending, pushing and pinching the plasticine. It is important to check that the ends of the wire are in the correct position on the stubs not only from the side but also from the end elevation (presuming that you have put the cup on its rest with the stubs at the highest point.)

By now the blob of glue at each end will have coalesced and probably run all over the place. This does not matter. Using the probe, drag up the lower portions and let them attach themselves to glue higher up the wire. There is absolutely no need to try and smooth the glue. The rougher it is the more keys there are for the moulding material. The point to watch at this stage is that there is actually glue all round the wire. The ideal application of the glue is shown in (Plate 9), but this only saves you the trouble of paring off the excess during the semi-set stage with a blade. If you are sure that the wire is in the correct position, put the piece aside until the glue is set. You can speed up the process under the lamp, but do not put the cup so close to the bulb that the heat softens the plasticine.

5. When the glue is set, remove the plasticine carefully, if necessary with a knife. Lift the cup up by its new wire handle to see if everything is in order. If some of the epoxy has flowed over the edge of the stubs, pare it off with a razor blade. Nowhere should the glue lie beyond the perimeter of the stub.

6. Except in the case of very small objects, Barbola can rarely be applied in one go. Usually two or three applications are necessary. Two layers, each $\frac{1}{8}''$ thick, applied successively, will dry to a hard condition twice as fast as one layer $\frac{1}{4}''$ thick.

Dig out sufficient putty-hard Barbola from the tin and roll it into a sausage in the palm of the left hand with the first and second fingers of the right hand. On a piece of glass cut the sausage with a knife to the approximate length of the handle, and roll this piece in a few drops of water on the glass plate. The diameter of the sausage should be less than the diameter of the finished handle, because at least one more layer is to be added. Run wet fingers along the wire and small drops of water will remain in the key marks. Place the Barbola along the wire and then pinch it round the wire with moistened fingers. No attempt should be made at this stage to smooth it, only to remove large bumps with a small pair of scissors. Any excess can be returned to the Barbola tin, and the lid should be replaced as soon as possible. If the wire is not covered, or if there are deep depressions, add a little more Barbola. Put the cup aside to dry. Do not try the lamp technique with wet Barbola because it is likely to form crevasses. If you are really in a hurry, a shelf over a radiator or the top of a central heating plant is a good drying place. (See Plate 10.)

7. When the Barbola is dry examine the handle very carefully, to see how much must be added as a second coat. Then moisten the dried out surface very carefully with one finger. Gradually build the handle up to the size and shape you require by adding suitably sized strips. Smooth the new into the old. A moistened finger is the best tool at this stage. It is possible to achieve a very smooth surface in this way, but do not overdo the water or the mixture flows away as a thin soup, leaving depressions. A small pool of this soup can appear to have a solid surface, but when it dries out there will be a depression. Allow the skin of the Barbola to harden and then add some more. (See Plate 11.)

During this smoothing stage there is one point which is particularly important, and is illustrated in Fig. 16. The Barbola should be made to flow over each stub and not stop short in a step.

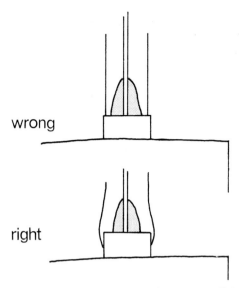

wrong

right

Fig. 16

8. Allow the Barbola to dry out until it is rock hard. On further examination you may find that a depression has formed or a pimple appeared. The former must be treated with a further addition, as in section 7 above, and the latter with a file or sandpaper. The underneath of the handle, i.e.: the side nearest to the cup itself, is usually the part that needs the most sandpaper treatment. It is at this stage that the greatest care must be taken. The slightest unevenness in the surface will show up very clearly after painting, so you must be quite sure that the surface is completely smooth. (See Plate 12.)

9. The foregoing repair could have been effected equally well with epoxy putty or Seelmasta. The result would have been the same, but the work would have taken longer and cost more. The method differs in that you should make only one application of the putty on the wire and, once it has hardened, the actual shaping has to be done with blade, file and wet-and-dry paper.

The finishing and painting of repairs such as those described above are detailed in Chapter 6.

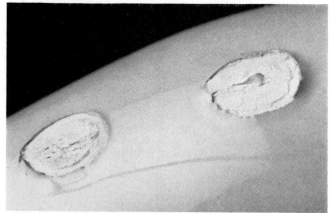

Plate 8

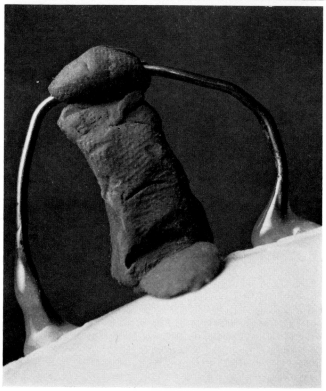

Plate 9

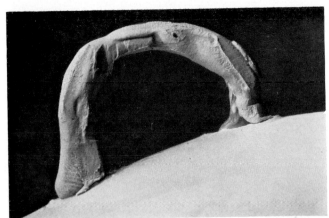

Plate 10

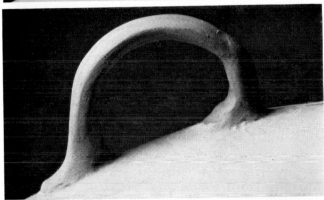

Plate 11

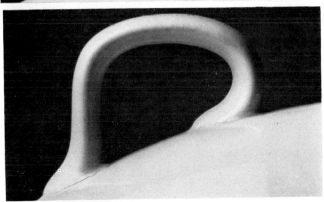

Plate 12

43

CHAPTER FIVE

MODELLING

It is not necessary that you take a night class in sculpture, but some ability to shape in the round is necessary. Before attempting to mould anything more artistic than a cup handle, some practice is advisable. The best way is to model some Barbola on the end of a matchstick, or a skewer if the object to be modelled is larger. If you are going to mend broken ornaments, the list of things you may have to model is endless; birds, flowers, fingers, hands, animals' legs, angels' wings, musical instruments, cows' horns, etc. Getting the proportions right is perhaps the most difficult problem. It is better, of the two, to make something too small than too large, because it is easier to add Barbola than to cut it away. Use the same technique as described in the last chapter.

If you are trying to match an object—for instance, if you are trying to replace a hand and the other hand is there for you to copy—it is comparatively easy, but sometimes you will meet the quite serious problem of not knowing what a hand was holding before it was broken. Reference to illustrated books on china in the local public library may give you the exact answer. On the other hand I have found that if one lives with a broken figure for, say, a fortnight, one somehow understands what the original artist had in mind. On two separate occasions I have put a broken figure on a side table, glancing at it every time I passed it, until eventually I knew what was missing. In the first case, the figure was a five inch high female, clothed in what appeared to be a hunting costume, including a hat with a feather in it. Her left hand was hanging loosely by her side, whilst the right hand was broken off at the wrist, the upper arm tight to the body and the forearm out straight and parallel to the ground. The question was, what had the missing hand been holding. The answer was, a hooded falcon. The other case was a beautiful Dresden figure, twelve inches high, of the goddess Ceres. The hand and half the right forearm were missing. The arm was well away from the body and had been holding something bulky as there was a mark of attachment in the position of the right collar bone. Two little cherubs were working a plough by her left foot, against a background of sheaves of corn. There was a basket of apples on the ground near her right foot. Eventually I made a cornucopia, overflowing with purple grapes, which reached from above her shoulder to her hip. Some time later I found this figure of Ceres in a book—complete with cornucopia. The only difference was that unfortunately my cornucopia had a left hand spiral whilst the original was right handed. (Plate 13.)

Plate 13

Pieces can be moulded separately from the figure and stuck on afterwards, or moulded in their final position. Missing flowers, and most small objects where the join is not visible, should be made separately, but in cases where the join will be visible it is better to work in the final position. Otherwise, when you have finished the modelling, the new piece must be held, epoxy glue applied to the stub, the piece pushed gently into position and then supported until it has hardened. There is naturally some danger of damaging the modelling you have taken so much care with.

You can apply the cup handle technique to the replacement of a missing leg on the figure of a dog, as illustrated in (Fig. 17.) The thickness of the piece of wire should correspond roughly to the size of the bone in the dog's leg, the function of which it is going to fulfil. Bend the wire so that the joints will be in the right place. Otherwise, proceed as before.

When making flowers you will probably find, unless they are very small, that it is best to make them petal by petal. Place the centre of the flower, in the shape of a ball, on a glass plate. Surround it with a ring of plasticine to support each petal as it is added. (See Fig. 10.) This will prevent the flower from looking mechanical and will give it life. Roll and flatten out the Barbola to

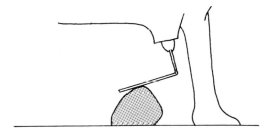

Fig. 17

petal thickness, cut to shape, and, with a blade or palette knife, ease it off the glass plate to which it has possibly stuck. Pick up each petal with the point of a pin at its base and transfer it to its position round the sphere. When all the petals are in position, take the dentist's tool and press the petal bases into the sphere, which now becomes a flat disc.

In the case of the cow and calf in the photograph (Plate 14a), the boscage at the back was completely missing and this had to be built up in stages.

Plate 14a   Plate 14b

The Chelsea Derby cow and calf in 14b served as the model for the reconstruction of the Derby cow and calf, 14a, which was bought for 2/6 in 20 pieces in a paper bag. The whole of the boscage had to be made (see text). The plasticine support slipped during hardening which accounts for the attack of rickets in the cow's front leg.

1.   Heavy brass wires were cut so that they would stop short of the tip of the outermost leaf, about $\frac{3}{4}''$ short, except in the downward direction, towards the trunk. The tips were supported by plasticine while the cross members were glued to the vertical member (Fig. 18) and allowed to harden. For the result of this first step see (Fig. 19).

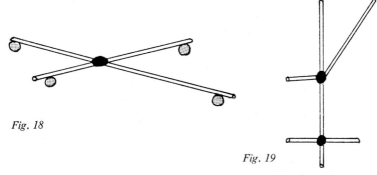

Fig. 18

Fig. 19

2. I then had the choice of gluing the downward piece to the existing tree trunk and carrying out the rest of the work in position, or working in the hand and sticking the result to the tree afterwards. As I was working on the cow at the same time, I chose the latter course.

3. The wires were then covered with Barbola and roughly smoothed to form branches. The Barbola was allowed to harden. (See Fig. 20.)

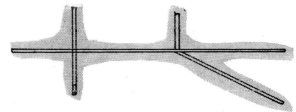

Fig. 20

4. Barbola, of a suitable consistency to be pressed out into thin pieces on a glass surface, was cut into approximately leaf shaped pieces which were separated one from another. (See Fig. 21.)

Fig. 21

5. With a modelling tool (a piece of wood, ivory or steel, pointed at one end and blunt at the other) the individual leaves were made; all similar but not identical. (See Fig. 22.)

Fig. 22

6. A very thin sausage of Barbola, wetted and lifted with a pin, was placed along the centre of some of the leaves and pushed into the surface to represent a vein. (See Fig. 23.)

Fig. 23

7. When the work was dry enough to handle without risk of distortion, the underside of the bottom of each leaf was thoroughly wetted, as was also the position of attachment on the branch, and the leaf applied with light pressure. (See Fig. 24.)

Fig. 24

8. The leaves were applied working from the outside towards the centre, each leaf slightly overlapping the previous one, the general formation of a tree borne in mind

9. Leaves were also applied to the back of the boscage in a similar manner, in nearly identical positions, so that the wetted backs of the leaves attached themselves to each other at certain points. This gave added strength to the whole structure.

10. When this stage was finished, the bottom of the vertical wire was attached to the stub with a large blob of epoxy glue. When this was hard, the main stem of the wire was covered with Barbola to form the trunk.

11. The bottom right leaves were thoroughly wetted to allow them to be bent and draped naturally over the cow's back.

12. When the work was dry all small prominences were rubbed down with sandpaper and smoothed with a wet paint brush.

13. The final stage was finishing and colouring, which whole subject is covered in the next chapter.

CHAPTER SIX

FINISHING

White—Other Colours

By finishing I mean colouring, and possibly varnishing, over a repair.

WHITE

This is by far the most difficult of all colours to match. I was once told that there were seventeen shades of white, each quite distinct from all the others. There are two different ways of applying white and I will detail both, although I prefer the second method.

1. Flake White in powder form should be well mixed with a few drops of picture varnish, on a piece of glass with a palette knife, until no trace of solid particles remain. Alternatively, Flake White squeezed from a student artists' tube requires less varnish. In either case the next step is to add a few drops of white spirit. It is never possible to state exact quantities, mixing colour and varnish in this way must necessarily be a matter of trial and error and of experience. Remember that the finished paint should not be so thin that it flows off a rounded surface and does not cover the object, nor should it be so thick that it is dragged with the brush when applied. Apply it evenly over the surface and put it aside to dry, which it does quickly because the white spirit is very volatile. In all probability you will need to cover a surface newly modelled in Barbola. It is therefore as well to apply a second coat of white, first adding a little more white spirit if the paint has begun to thicken, before attempting to mix the exact tint of white you need. In this way, the darker colour of the moulding material will be completely hidden and there will be no risk of it showing through the final coat.

For the third and final coat mix some more Flake White as before and then begin to add very small quantities of whichever colour you believe will give you the shade you want. More often than not this will be yellow ochre. It is as well to push some of the white to one side with the palette knife before you begin to add the colour. If you find you have overdone the colour you can pull back some of the untouched white to correct the tint.

It is important to test the shade by making a small brush stroke on the figure on a patch of the colour you are trying to match. If you find it very hard to see, you have done well. If it is too obvious, leave it there, adjust the colour of the paint, and make another brush stroke alongside the first. When you have achieved a good match, remove the test strokes with white spirit and apply the colour lightly with a soft brush. Particular care must be taken at this point because if there is too much white spirit in your mixture, or if you apply too much pressure, you will damage the existing undercoats of white.

As I have already pointed out, the addition of the white spirit is critical and it is important to remember that it evaporates very quickly and that its evaporation has the effect of making the paint thicker. If for any reason you have to break off your work for five minutes, scrape the paint into a heap and cover it with a small dish or the lid of a tin.

This final coat must be applied with great care, using a feathering technique. By this I mean bring any excess paint from within the area to be covered over the join and on to the original china, reducing the pressure on the brush as you do so.

As soon as the job is finished, clean brushes, palette knife and glass with white spirit.

2. The second method, which I prefer, is to use cellulose lacquers or car-touch-up-paints. This method

is simpler because no colour mixing is involved, but naturally there are disadvantages as well as advantages and I think it will be helpful if I list both.

Disadvantages

1. The containers are not ideal, and it is vital that the threads around the lids are kept clear of paint.

2. They dry far too quickly for other colours to be mixed with them for exact matching of a tint, which is why it is necessary to have a variety of shades of white in stock.

3. The volume that one has to buy in these containers is too great.

Advantages

1. They dry more quickly than other paints.

2. They resist water and most solvents, except acetone.

3. They give a brilliant porcelain-like glow.

4. However roughly they are applied they settle down by themselves into a beautifully smooth surface.

5. They do not discolour with age in the way that many paints do.

OTHER COLOURS

If necessary colour can be applied to a white base as soon as it is ready. Naturally, if you intend to apply colour the exact shade of the white base is relatively unimportant. All that is required is that it should not be too dark and should cover the grey tone of the moulding material. I cannot, unfortunately, recommend the use of *coloured* cellulose lacquers. The range of colours available is too limited, and too crude, and they dry far too quickly to be blended with each other or with other colouring agents.

If you have used the first method, described above, to apply the white base, you should proceed as follows:

Use picture varnish for a base and add the necessary colour or colours from the tubes of student artists' paints, mixing with a palette knife on a piece of glass. You may be involved in considerable trial and error until you find the right tone. Considering the relatively tiny amount of paint you are going to apply this is a very wasteful operation so try to work with minimum quantities. Do not forget to use long brush strokes, the feathering technique described earlier, and the fact that white spirit should be added drop by drop to give the paint the right consistency. Do not add the white spirit until you are ready to use the paint. Two or more coats of colour may be necessary and, when they are thoroughly dry, apply a thin coat of picture varnish, without white spirit, over the whole area to reproduce the effect of glazing.

If you are applying colour to a white cellulose lacquer base, you should proceed exactly as above, simply omitting the final coat of picture varnish. Also, be very careful to avoid using acetone when removing colour-test strokes.

The thinner the coat with which you achieve the final colour, the quicker it will dry. It is probable, too, that humidity affects drying time. You would be wise to assume that the final coat will take at least a day to dry out fully.

THE RIGHT COLOUR

Once again I am forced to say that you will learn by experience how to match colours. But the following basic hints will be useful:

1. Flesh tint is a standard colour but it is invariably suitable only for cherubs' cheeks. Usually it has to be toned down with yellow ochre and/or white.

2. Vegetation (leaves, boscage etc.) varies between dark green and greenish yellow. Any tone can be easily reached by mixing viridian green with chrome yellow or yellow ochre. This seems an easier way than mixing blue and yellow.

3. If any blend of colours appears to be too bright, the tone can be made duller by the addition of small quantities of Burnt Sienna or Payne's Grey. This latter is useful for toning white to the colour often found in Chinese porcelain—a sort of blue grey.

4. The crackle on Chinese vases can be reproduced by a well sharpened H pencil, after practising the crackle design first on a piece of paper. Alternatively, scratch the painted surface, when thoroughly dry, with the point of a needle and then rub Vandyck brown into the scratches with one finger.

5. If you have to touch up a face on a piece of antique china, remember to use brown paint for the eyes. No blue eyes appeared on porcelain figures before 1850.

6. Biscuit is the name given to unglazed porcelain and here one runs into real trouble because the varnish used for applying the paints themselves will always have a sheen and the repair will appear glazed. It is possible to mix the paint with white spirit only, but the adhesion is not so good in this case. I found one solution when I was trying to repair the handle of a small Wedgwood urn. Wedgwood porcelain is often unglazed and in this case was a strong violet blue. The trick I used was to blend the colours from the tubes (red and ultramarine) and roll the result into epoxy glue/kaolin putty. Thus, however much the handle was shaped and rubbed down, the matching colour was always there. If you try this,

you will find that you need to use a great deal of colour.

7.   Missing pieces of coloured glass can be filled in by colouring German epoxy glue—Uhu Special—and letting the glue settle into the hole, which must be backed by a piece of sellotape to prevent the thin glue from running out at the back. Once the glue is hardened it is possible to pull off the tape. If it does not come off easily it is quite safe to dissolve it away with any one of the common solvents. They will not affect the hardened epoxy glue.

8.   Before applying a gold line to a cup or figure, paint in a line of Indian red first. This gives the gold a stronger glow.

Finally, do make notes of the colours you have mixed to obtain specific results, and do wait for daylight before attempting even the simplest colour match.

CHAPTER SEVEN

AFTERTHOUGHTS

1. Do not refuse any small job. These techniques are applicable to most jobs, even mending model ships.

2. Put screw tops back on glue tubes at once. If interchanged, the result can be calamitous.

3. If you don't clean paint brushes after use you will have to buy new ones—and good ones are expensive.

4. When you select a brush for use, check with finger and thumb that the hairs are soft. If they are hard and stuck together don't force them apart or some of them will snap. Keep a bottle of old mixed solvents on the worktable and soak the brush in this mixture for two or three minutes or until the hairs are softened.

5. If you don't want the trouble of cleaning up a colour palette with an old cloth, mix the colours on a piece of broken window glass and throw it away after use.

6. Do not try to work on the lip of a tall vase when the vase is standing on a bench. Place it on a firm box on the floor, bringing the lip to normal working height.

7. Don't put newly repaired pieces on the floor—it is too easy to drop tools on them or to step on them.

8. If you have to improve a figure which has a badly stuck on head or limb, hold it under the hot tap

with the water flowing over the join in question. Do not immerse the whole figure in a basin of hot water unless you are positive there are no other joins in it.

9. Put unused Barbola back in its tin. Make odd flowers, etc., with residues of epoxy putty. Unused epoxy glue, on the other hand, should be disposed of.

10. Small dropping bottles, from a chemist, are excellent when small quantities of alcohol or white spirit are to be added to a mixture.

11. It is wise to have two rags so that there is always a clean one available.

12. Remember that Plasticine and a used Ever Ready safety razor blade are the most invaluable of all the tools at your disposal.

13. Ordinary safety razor blades are less dangerous when broken lengthwise, and will trim curved surfaces better.

14. Second hand books on china with lots of illustrations, and even cuttings from newspapers and magazines, can be very helpful if you are trying to decide on the correct shape of a missing piece.

15. A silver object can be moulded or worked from shellac. Melt the shellac in an old kitchen spoon with aluminium powder stirred into it.

16. Small chips out of alabaster figures or bases can be replaced with beeswax. Put a piece of beeswax onto the broken place. Heat a probe in a gas flame. When you touch the beeswax with the heated probe it will melt and fill the cavity. Trim excess with a blade. Note that if you heat the probe in a candle flame the beeswax will be marked with soot.

17. Epoxy putty, coloured with Yellow Ochre, is a good match for ivory.

18. Repair papier maché trays with Isopon, painted over with black cellulose paint.

19. Irish Belleek china has a most unusual glaze. Mother-of-pearl nail varnish is a good match.

20. If you are trying to match white bisque or parian ware, neither of which have a covering white glaze, use Devcon 2 Ton—Kaolin—and wash your hands thoroughly before using the material, to keep it white.

21. A useful probe for testing for steps in joins, and removing excess glue from them, can be made quite easily. Bore a small hole in a piece of wood, to form a handle, glue a needle, eye first, into the hole, using an epoxy glue. Make sure that about $\frac{2}{3}$ of the needle remain sticking out.

CHAPTER EIGHT

TRUE TALE OF A CHINA REPAIRER

A few years ago a china repairer was working in the dingy window of his shop in London when an elderly gentleman entered, carrying a paper parcel.

"Could you please mend my valuable Roman vase?" he said.

"Yes, certainly."

"How much will it cost?"

The repair would have consisted of a dab of molten shellac, a rub down and a coat of paint—perhaps fifteen minutes work.

"Half-a-crown—please call again on Saturday."

The repairer put the Roman vase on the seat of the only other chair in the shop and continued to work. Ten minutes later his father and partner came in and sat on the chair.

When they had calmed down, the pieces of the Roman vase were swept up with great care with a dustpan and brush.

On Saturday the owner came to collect his repaired vase.

"I am very sorry," said the china mender, "that your vase is not ready, but my father and I had to shut the shop all this week and carry out some urgent work for the British Museum. Please call next Saturday."

On the following Saturday the repairer used a different technique. "I am very sorry, but my father was doing the job and he is in bed with bronchitis. Please call next Saturday."

On the third Saturday the elderly gentleman enquired for his Roman vase.

"Which vase was that?" said the china mender.

"The valuable Roman one, green, with a chip in the neck."

"Ah yes. I had forgotten it for the moment. Here it is. Shall I wrap it up? That's half-a-crown. Thank you."

"Thank you very much," said the gentleman. "How beautifully your father has repaired it. I cannot see where the chip was."